WHAT A COINCIDENCE

By FRANK TRACY

Copyright © 2015 by Frank Tracy

What a Coincidence
by Frank Tracy

Printed in the United States of America.

ISBN 9781498437936

All rights reserved solely by the author. The author guarantees all contents are original and do not infringe upon the legal rights of any other person or work. No part of this book may be reproduced in any form without the permission of the author. The views expressed in this book are not necessarily those of the publisher.

Unless otherwise indicated, Scripture quotations taken from the King James Version (KJV) – *public domain.*

Order additional copies at mft5@juno.com

Or contact the author at P O Box 896 Byron, Georgia 31008

www.xulonpress.com

Contents

Introduction vii

Chapter 1: It begins 9
Chapter 2: Trouble in paradise 11
Chapter 3: On our own 13
Chapter 4: Getting a job 19
Chapter 5: A new Daddy 23
Chapter 6: Some wonderful people 25
Chapter 7 well what do you think 29
Chapter 8: Our mother 31
Chapter 9: Found out 33
Chapter 10: A whole new life 37
Chapter 11: What did I do? 39
Chapter 12: A life change 43
Chapter 13: A new home 47
Chapter 14: Move to Orlando 49
Chapter 15: The florist shops 53
Chapter 16: redoing vows and churches 57
Chapter 17: Child evangelism Fellowship 63
Chapter 18: new commitment 67
Chapter 19: Heartbreak and a new beginning 69
Chapter 20: God's Grace 73
Chapter 21: The beginning 77

Introduction

I was born on a cold November 20th 1941 in the late afternoon. My father was away in the United States Army somewhere in the Philippines Islands. I was certainly too young to remember, but all heck was about to break loose out there in the Pacific as the Empire of Japan was about to attack Pearl Harbor in Hawaii.

By the time I was old enough to remember anything, my father had come home from where he had been freed from a Japanese prison camp on Manila. At least this is what I was told later on in life. While a prisoner he had become very ill with Black Fever and Malaria and almost died. We were living in Peoria Illinois at the time because they had a large Army hospital there, and my father was at the time I am referring to, still an outpatient.

My mother was pregnant with what was to become my little brother Billy. I did have a little sister Molly, who was two. I also had an older brother Richard age 6. I did not realize it at the time but Richard was severely retarded. My name is Frank and I was 4 years old.

I need to tell you right up front that I have cut the word coincidence out of my dictionary, along with the word luck. Over the years I have learned something so strong and powerful that I feel compelled to share it by telling this story. I believe that there is no such thing as coincidence, there is only God. When you read this story I believe you will agree.

Chapter 1

We were renting part of a two story house. The landlady lived upstairs and we had the downstairs. One day I was playing with some friends and Richard. The landlady had been cleaning the entranceway and the wooden stairs. She had somehow left a carton of Lewis Lye on the stairs. We as children of course found it. We thought it might be sugar. You would think that what followed would have broken me from always being the one dumb enough to try anything once, but it didn't. I volunteered to taste it. I took a rather large handful of what I thought was sugar and gulped it down. Oh my, it began to burn like fire in my throat and stomach. I screamed and ran to where my mother was in the kitchen. "Help me Mommy, It burns, it burns", I cried. When she found out what I had done she lovingly did the worst thing she could do, she mixed up a concoction of milk and lard to make me vomit. "Quick" she said "drink all of this down, it will get the poison out." All it did was to give the lye a second chance to recoat my throat. I was still screaming and crying when just a few moments later my father, who had just left the hospital, came in. He quickly found out what was wrong, picked me up and ran out of the house to where a trolley car was. He was yelling back to my mother "meet us at the hospital as soon as you can."

He yelled to the trolley car driver, "Wait for us my son has swallowed poison and needs to go to the hospital." When he quickly explained to the trolley driver, the driver told everyone to "hang on were going to the hospital". He made the trolley go as fast as it would go clanging the bell all the way so that others could get out of the way. I remember that ride as if it was just minutes ago. I was in agony and my daddy was holding and trying to comfort me. That may be one of the reasons I never came to hate my father for what he did to us later on. All I could do was scream and cry. I wonder if people today would be so helpful.

What a coincidence, my father coming in, the trolley car being there, and the tracks running to the front of the hospital. All of these things together are what saved my life. When they got me to the hospital they quickly pumped out my stomach and then for whatever reason put me into a tub full of ice and water. I was in the hospital over a week and was fed a lot of Jell-O, ice cream and lots and lots of goat's milk. My guess is that the Tracy family became quite well known there because; Billy was born while I was there, my father was an outpatient and me in for being not too smart. I guess all that goat's milk must have worked though because I'm still here. I remember all of this so well, and I'm sure it's because of the severe pain the lye caused.

Chapter 2

I remember a lot of typical childish things that took place over the next several months. I was home, so was my mother and my new little brother, and my father had been discharged from the hospital and the army. Mostly I remember my mom and dad fighting and arguing a lot. I guess the reasons are obvious now as I look back. Mom and dad decided to move back to Davenport Iowa where I had been born. My father was drinking a lot more now, and so was my mother. My father had a favorite way of driving my mother crazy. He had been blessed with the ability to play just about any kind of musical instrument and when he would come home drunk he would get on the piano and play the song they sang as the ship Titanic was sinking, "Nearer my God to Thee". It would make her so mad but he sometimes would just keep playing it over and over again. By the way, it drove us all crazy. It didn't seem to matter to either of them what they were doing to their kids. At first we tried to make them stop fighting by begging them to stop. "Please stop, please," we would beg, but to no avail. We had a favorite place where we would get together and hide when they got like this, and believe me it was very often. My father, if possible became even worse. He drank all the time now. Who knows maybe it was a blessing because he stayed away more and more.

I was 6 years old and I will never forget the day he pulled up in front of the house we were renting. He had a strange woman in the car with him. He got out of the car carrying an empty suitcase, came into the house and packed his clothes. What took place, and what was said, between mom and dad is not repeatable. Despite the crying and begging from all of us kids; "please daddy, please don't go. Daddy we love you please don't go", he left anyhow. As he left he turned and said to us, "I don't think any of you are my kids. Go find your real dad". We ran to our mother and begged her to "make him stop," All she said was, "let him go, he's no good anyhow." That was the last time I ever heard of or saw my father. At least I never heard from him again. Billy found out about him and where he was many years later and went to see him. He lived in Utah with a wife and children. He was a member of the Mormon Church and I guess respected in his community. I had no desire to see him or make a claim on anything he had. I did not hate him, I just didn't care.

Chapter 3

My mother didn't handle any of this very well. She began to drink more and began hanging out with a lot of different men at many different bars. She became less and less concerned about her children. By the time I was 8 years old we were pretty much left to fend for ourselves. Somehow deep down inside I felt an obligation to take care of my brothers and sister. I taught myself how to cook a lot of different things, how to do laundry, including iron. I seemed to know the importance of keeping us all clean and fed. I do remember one thing that didn't work out so well. "Make us a cake," molly said. "a chocolate one' Billy said." I gathered all of the ingredients in the cook book and mixed them up just like it said, or so I thought, it looked pretty good. The surprise came when we tried to eat it. "It tastes like sand" Molly said. "Yea" said Billy "it's terrible". You know what? It did taste like sand. That was the last of my cake baking days.

Even back then we would get hungry because our mother was often too busy elsewhere. We devised ways to make a little money so we could buy something to eat. Of course we bought junk food, but at least it was something. I had told all of the kids to pick up any bottles that we could sell. Even beer bottles were worth a penny each. I had also found out you could make money selling copper so I told them to pick up any copper wire they found. It seemed there was always a lot of wire in junk piles. We would burn the rubber coating off and roll it into a ball. When the ball was big enough we would sell it at the junk yard. It had become obvious to me by then that my older brother simply would not be much help due to his mental condition and that it was my responsibility to take care of us all. Even then our Father in Heaven was looking out for us.

Finally it happened, our mother hadn't come home for well over two weeks. We looked all over town for her but could not find her. I don't think I need to explain to you how frightened we were. What were we going to do? She must have known what she was doing because before she disappeared she did stock the pantry. In my heart and mind I knew from what had happened to other families, that if we reported this to the police we would be separated and placed in different homes or worse. We all agreed not to tell anyone and to stick together.

That Saturday morning the landlord came to the door demanding to see our mom and get his rent money. "Where is your mother" he said loudly. "She's at work" I lied. He made it clear that the rent was way late and if he didn't get it we were going to be thrown out. I told him I would tell her as soon as she got home. Molly started crying, "where's mommy we need her where is she"? That started Billy crying. I had to stop feeling sorry for myself and comfort the two of them. "It well be ok", I said. I didn't have the slightest idea at the time what we would do but I wanted to stop them from crying so I said "tomorrow morning we are going to find us a new place to live, A place they can't throw us out of. We are going to be fine as long as we have each other".

"Do you promise Frank? Do you". Molly asked. I said "I sure do promise and it's going to be fun for us". Molly and Billy stopped crying and we gave each other a big hug. "I Love you guys" I said. "We love you too", Molly and Billy said at the same time. I wondered what are we were going to do now.

What could an eight year old boy with a little sister age 6, a brother age 4, and an older brother who was less mature than either of the little ones, possibly do? Well you might be surprised. All I knew at that moment was that something had to be done.

Then I remembered seeing an old fishing shack that had been abandoned down in the woods by the Mississippi River that myself, and a couple of friends had run into one day when we were out exploring around. What if? It was in a very desolate and lonely spot in the woods next to the river. I went the next morning to check it out: the shack was still there, it would require a lot of work but I thought that it could be made into a place to live.

We made a total of three trips of almost three miles each way to get everything we could move to the shack. Every one of those trips was hard,

Chapter 3

each time we carried as much as we could and put the heavy stuff on our wagon. I really don't know how we made it. We stopped and took a lot of breaks. It was little Billy that needed the most help, he was only four. They were sure glad when I said "this is the last trip guys, we can make it; can't we?" "Yea" they shouted, "the last one for real?" Molly asked. I answered "for real, I promise." School had just let out for the summer so we had plenty of time to get everything done. Isn't that a coincidence?

It took several days and a lot of hard work to clean the mud off the floor and clean up everything else. Getting set up was quite a job, including standing up the old outhouse over a new hole, but we did it. That outhouse was a blessing but we sure hated it in the winter. We made the place livable, at least by our standards and I think that we did it well. I remember Molly saying to me," I'm tired can we sleep now"? I'll never forget the look on her face. She had worked so hard. "Sure we can you have earned a rest". Richard (Dick) took a little coaxing but he did his share, especially helping move that outhouse. It was summer when we moved in. So the weather was in our favor. Everything came together for us, another coincidence.

Our new home had two rooms, a small bed room and the other, I guess you would call it, a great room. The large room had a kitchen type counter with a sink and a hand pump that worked. There was no kitchen stove but there was an old ice box in pretty good shape. In the center of the large room was a big iron stove that burned wood or coal. We used that stove for everything, cooking, heat, water for baths and laundry, even to heat the flat iron for ironing. You name it that stove did it. It was hot in the summer but we had to cook on it for a long time before we found a two burner kerosene table top stove. That little kerosene stove worked great.

We used the small room for a bedroom for Molly and to store some of the different supplies we had. We set up a corner of the big room as a bed room for us boys. I remember Dick getting a little upset because Molly had her own room but I somehow got it across to him that she was a girl and that we were boys and she needed to have her own room.

One of the most important things we had was a red Western Flyer wagon. That wagon was a true blessing. It hauled a lot of stuff when we had moved. We found an old washing machine that someone had put on the curb to be picked up by the trash man. We loaded it on the wagon and brought it home. We didn't have electric so we couldn't plug it in, it probably wouldn't have worked anyhow, but it had a tub that we could use to wash our clothes in and a drain on the bottom that made it easy to change the water. More importantly it had a hand cranked wringer on it. Anyone who has ever done laundry by hand would know what a blessing it was to have that wringer. It's a lot of work to do it by hand. With the ringer the clothes would even dry faster on the line. Laundry was mostly my job. There was no sense in doing laundry if you didn't get the clothes clean.

Wood for the stove began to get harder and harder to find. One day our search for wood took us to the railroad tracks. The tracks were about 2 blocks distance from the shack. This was a time in history when trains ran by steam engines, fueled by coal. We noticed pieces of coal laying on the tracks. So we began to collect it in our wagon. The farther we went in one direction the more coal we found. About a half mile down the tracks was a round house. For those of you who don't know, a round house is a large building that is built to turn on a huge swivel. This one had 4 sets of tracks inside going in towards the middle. When a steam locomotive would need service or repair they would drive it into the round house and do the required work. This one was built to hold up to 4 locomotives at a time by pulling one in, turning the building to an empty set of tracks and pull in another as needed. When the locomotive was ready to leave they would fill the hopper with coal. As it was leaving, the engine would bounce around a lot switching from one set of tracks to another and spill out some of the coal. We would come along with our wagon and pick up the coal for our stove. We stockpiled a lot of coal all summer long. Because of this we never ran out of fuel for our stove. What a coincidence.

As summer came to an end I thought that we needed to go to school if we were ever going to learn anything. Also I thought we might get spotted pretty quickly if we were not in school. To tell the truth I don't know why I thought this way, it certainly made things a lot more difficult, but as I look back I am sure glad I did. At least we all got a good education those years we were together. Billy was too young for school that year, but the rest of us needed to go. I want to tell you now, looking back, Billy was a real trooper. As far as I know He did everything he was asked to do. I told him that during the day he should stay in the house with the door locked so that he would be safe. When I think back it brings tears to my eyes just thinking about how lonely and freighted he must have been. Just four years old, but as far as I know he did everything that he was asked to do. The closest school was a catholic school. So that's where we went. We worked it out so that their school bus picked us up on the road not far from our shack. It was surprisingly easy to forge the papers needed to get us enrolled and into the school. I don't have any idea of how many excuses we came up with over the next couple of years selling the fact that mom was always sick or had to work, you name it we used it, somehow we managed. I'm sure this was all a coincidence.

Chapter 4

Getting our lives together was quite a challenge from the beginning. But there was at least one other important item to address, we needed to eat. I pondered and worried a lot on how to take care of this problem. Obviously we needed money. I had to get a job. We had just gotten into our new home when we realized that the food we had brought with us was starting to run low. Realizing that I had to have a job I started looking. Almost immediately I found a job sitting pins in a bowling alley. It was hard work for an 8 year old but I learned real quick and pretty soon as was as good as any pin sitter there. I didn't think about the dangerous part of the job but I found out about it the hard way. I was sitting pins for two men who had been drinking quite a bit. One of the men threw his ball and hit only two pins. Doing my job I jumped down into the pit to send his ball back and pick up the two pins. Meanwhile he had taken his friends ball and thrown it down the alley. He got a lot of pins with that one and one of them hit me in the head knocking me out for a couple of minutes. The owner of the alley actually got mad at me and fired me. The man felt bad and gave me 5 dollars, but meanwhile I was out of work.

I was looking for another job. If you think about how we were living it should not surprise you when I say I knew my way around some. I had seen boys going into the back of the newspaper office and coming out with papers. I thought, maybe I could make some money selling papers. So I went in. There was a room with a big table, on the table were stacks of newspapers, each stack had 20 papers in it. You had to pay 50 cents for a stack and then go sell the twenty papers for a dollar. Why not give it a try, I thought.

I tried it for a few days and realized that I wasn't making anywhere near enough money. I racked my brain trying to figure a way. One afternoon a thought came into my head and for some reason, carrying my papers. I went into a skid row bar walking through slowly saying "extra, extra, read all about it in today's paper". Sometimes I would say "Extra, Extra, read all about it, big hole in the ocean, Mississippi on fire". A man sitting at the bar turned and asked me "boy how many papers have you got?" I told him "20." He then threw me a silver dollar and told me, "keep the papers but get out of the bar, this is no place for a kid." I was polite and responded, "Thank you sir for the money, but I need to make some money so we can eat". Then two other men and a women each gave me a dollar. Wow, this works I thought. I thanked them and left. I had found a way to make money selling papers. In Davenport Iowa it seemed like there was a bar on every corner, sometimes 3 or 4 in a row. Later on I even went across the river to Rock Island, Moline and East Moline to the many bars there. That way I wasn't wearing out a good thing in just a few bars. I found out that an 8 year old boy in a bar trying to sell papers to make money to eat got a lot of good response. What a coincidence.

Well we had money, but an 8 year old boy can't sign a lease or sign up for electric. So we still had to make do with our shack. We managed to acquire two kerosene lamps to use at night and we found a kerosene heater to put into Molly's room at night in the winter. We used a great many candles. One of the things we did that makes me wonder to this day is this, we drank the water from that hand pump at the sink. Just a thought, we never even thought about bad water. We used that water for just about everything. But think about it: A shallow well just a few feet from one of the dirtiest rivers in the world, that muddy filthy Mississippi River and we never got sick from the water. It almost had to be poison, and we lived there for well over two years. What a coincidence.

"I'm scared" Molly cried. "It's dark in here and I heard a noise outside." I pulled her close to me and said "you don't have to be afraid we're all here to protect you." "Let me turn the lamp up a little." "Will you tell us a story Frank, please?" Molly asked. "What story do you want me to tell you?" "Any story", she said, "they're all good". "Yea" said Billy "tell us a story". Even Dick liked the stories, he never said it but he listened to all of them. That night I told them the story of The Three Little Pigs. In a short time after we had settled in there I had memorized every fairy tell story

Chapter 4

and poem there was. I also read them several books. Books like Treasure Island or Black Beauty. Looking back I realize how important it was to me to see even one smile on their faces.

"I'm not going out to get wood and you can't make me" Dick screamed. "Dick, you've got to do your share, everyone else does. That's how it works". "No I don't and I won't" he shouted. "If you don't get out there and get some wood I will have to punish you", I told him. "Uh Uh you can't cause I'm bigger than you" he said. We had been through this before. He was bigger and stronger, but his mental condition made him slower, so yes I could handle him. I really hated this whole situation, but I didn't know any other way to handle him at the time. I would get a head lock or some other hold on him and make him say uncle and then he would do as I asked.

Chapter 5

As I mentioned at the beginning, I was born in Davenport Iowa. It got dark very early in November in Iowa and it was often very cold. It was November 20 1950, my 9th birthday. I hadn't said anything to my brothers or sister. I was on my way home from selling papers and I was in the middle of a world class pity party. No mom to make me a cake, sing happy birthday etc. etc., you name it, I was really into this pity party. By coincidence I found myself walking at least two blocks out of my way and found myself standing in front of the Salvation Army Church. They were singing inside, and it looked warm. So I went in.

    I don't remember what the preacher preached that night but I sure do remember his invitation. When he finished I found myself running out the door with tears streaming down my cheeks. You see I understood just enough of what he was saying to know it did not include me. I couldn't be saved, I had done too many bad things already including, whatever I had done to make my mother and father leave us. I realized years later that this is the way a child's mind reasons. That has certainly been a blessing in these later years when I am comforting a child in similar circumstances.

    I didn't sleep that night. I cried a lot. Molly and Billy asked me what was wrong. I told them that I had hurt myself that day but that I would be fine tomorrow. There was no school the next day due to the Thanksgiving Holiday, that afternoon I headed to town to sell my papers. Somehow by coincidence on the way home I found myself in front of that Salvation Army Church again. I went inside again, as I was going in they were singing what has become my very favorite song, The Old Rugged Cross. Then the preacher began to preach (he was a captain) I didn't know it then but he was wearing two bars on his collar. He asked anyone who had a Bible to turn to the book of John, chapter one, verse twelve. As he read that verse somehow it began to burn into my memory for ever. He read it so loud and so clear.

"But as many as received Him, to them gave He power to become the sons of God. Even to them that believe on His name."

As he preached on that verse and explained it to us all, my heart began to warm. I so very badly needed and wanted a father. This time when he gave the invitation I was the first one down the aisle to ask Jesus into my heart. I had burst into happy tears as a very sweet and special older lady took my hand and helped me to understand and accept the Lord as my new Father. MY NEW DADDY! That wonderful lady explained to me that I had a father who would never leave me, not ever. Jesus said, "I will never leave you or forsake you" You know what? He never has. So you see I have two birthdays in a row. One on November 20, 1941 when I was born a baby boy, and one on Tuesday November 21, 1950 at 6:32PM, when I was born again as a son of God.

I'm sure I made that 3 mile walk home in record time. I was so happy and I wanted to share it with my family. They gave me a small New Testament Bible with Proverbs and Psalms in it. I still have it today. When I got home I told them what had happened and showed them the little Bible. I read John 1:12 to them and explained it the best I could. Many a night they would ask me to read from that small Bible so I started from the front and read to the back, explaining everything the best I could. I can't even to begin to relate to you how happy I was when many years later they told me that they had prayed together and asked Jesus into their hearts after I had read the Bible to them. Somehow life seemed so much better after Jesus found me. What a coincidence.

Chapter 6

The part of the Mississippi River that we lived on did not flow with a current. From the Iowa side to an island called Credit Island they had built a solid stone causeway. That causeway stopped the flow of the river on the Iowa side of Credit Island. Credit Island is a large island in the middle of the Mississippi River. The island to the best of my memory was about 3 miles long. Because of this, in the winter the ice between the island and the Iowa side of the river would freeze over so thick cars could drive on it. We had gotten ice skates from the Salvation Army store and had taught ourselves how to ice skate. We also figured out how to put a sail on a sled and ride the wind. There were a lot of happy hours out on the ice. In spring though, the river rose and there was a current then because the river overflowed the causeway. We were forced every spring to find high ground to camp out on until the water went down. Then we would have to clean up the muddy mess. We found an old wooden rowboat and managed to make it usable. We used it like a taxi from the road to our shack while the water was rising. We also used it to fish or row over to Credit Island, there was a park there and we would often go there to play There must have been an Indian battle of some kind there because we found a lot of arrow heads and tomahawk blades. We also found a few things we didn't recognize.

One day when we were fishing from our boat we met a black man, his name was Homer. Homer was very old (at least to us). He lived in a fishing shack about a mile downstream from us. We liked him right away, he liked us as well, and anyhow we got along fine and enjoyed each other's company. He taught us a lot of wonderful things. He taught us how to catch fish, and how to clean them. He showed me how to skin a rabbit or a squirrel, how to dress it and cook it. One of the things he taught me that I really liked was how to smoke fish. To this day I love good smoked fish. So many people were good to us. None of them knew that we had no parents, but somehow they knew to help us. For instance on my walk home from selling papers I passed a butcher shop, Sometimes I would go in and buy some meat, most of the time hamburger, it was only 20 cents a pound then for ground beef. It was as if the owner understood that we could use help. One day he asked, "Do you have a dog?" I told him "yes I do and my dogs name is DOG."

He laughed and said "would you mind if once in a while I gave you some dog bones to carry home to Dog"? "No" I said. "Wait here" he added and went into his cooler and came out with what he called a bag of dog bones. They had a lot of meat on them to be just dog bones. I'll tell you right now. They sure made some wonderful soup and stew. Dog still got the bones.

On terribly cold days there was a small restaurant that I passed every day selling papers. When I was really cold I would often go in and order a small 20 cent bowl of the best chili I ever ate. The owner's idea of small was to me a big bowl of chili. He also would give me all the oyster crackers that I wanted. I will never forget the warm and generous hearts of those men and others. What a coincidence.

We used the Salvation Army store a lot. We would find clothes, shoes, coats, even pots and pans. You name it and we found it there. One day as we were shopping there they were putting up posters advertising Vacation Bible School (VBS) "What do we need to do to come"? I asked the lady. "Just take this permission slip to your parents and have them sign it" she answered. I filled out the slips for all of us and brought them back.

That Vacation Bible School was one of the most fun things we ever got to do. They had wonderful stories and they had great snacks. Such as a lot of milk and cookies. And they even served a lunch because in those days VBS was an all-day affair. We attended VBS at the Salvation Army two years in a row. I like to believe that we also learned a lot about the Bible. To this day I have no doubt in my heart about the importance of Vacation Bile Schools and how they can impact the lives of children.

There was another even more wonderful thing they did. It was summer camp. The Salvation Army sponsored a two week camp. Your parents had

Chapter 6

to come down and ask, sign you up and then you could go to camp for free. The way I worked that out was to bring a letter that I had written from my mother saying that she was bed ridden and could not come down but could her son Frank bring the papers home and she would sign them. You know what? It worked. All 4 of us went to camp. Because of the age and boy girl thing we were separated into different cabins. We were still able to see each other a lot during the day, which was great because Billy and Molly were a little freighted. It didn't take them long to get over that and have a great time. For me it was like a two week vacation. Wonderful! We only went the one time, but as I said. It was great. I have always been very fond of the Salvation Army and all they do for the community.

Chapter 7

I'll bet your wondering by now. How could four little kids manage to do all of these things? It probably seems a little farfetched to you. Let me tell you it wasn't all easy. As a matter of fact there is no way that I could tell you everything that we went through. I couldn't afford the paper to write it all down on. But by the grace of God we made it. I know that God and by the way, his angels, were indeed looking after us. It seemed, no matter what the circumstances, He always provided the solution. When I asked He was always there with the answers. For instance, I remember a terrible incident that occurred. You can believe it or not. I'll certainly never forget it. One spring when the Mississippi had risen almost to the floor of our house, we were doing what silly children do. We were jumping off of our stoop into the river and having a good time. The weather was warm and we all could at least dog paddle by then. I had already jumped a few times and had climbed the steps to jump again. This time I landed on a one gallon glass bottle that had broken in half. It tore a large gash in my ankle. What do you do when you have no parents? No doctor to go to? I know that my Father in Heaven guided me thru this. It was bleeding a lot. I knew that I had to stop the bleeding so I said to Molly and Billy "bring me a towel" and then I asked Molly "please go get my sewing kit." Molly brought me the kit and I took out some black thread and a needle and I sewed up the cut as best I could until it stopped bleeding. To this day I do not know how or why I thought to do this, but I did. We had gotten a tin of Watkins black salve, which said to" put it on cuts", so I put a lot on the cut and wrapped it up in torn pieces of cloth. Every day I would clean the cut put on more Watkins salve and re wrap it. You know what?

It healed up. To this day I brag on that Watkins salve. My only answer to this is in the Bible.

In the Bible he asks in Mathew Chapter 6 verse 26 "Behold the fowls of the air: for they sow not, neither do they reap, nor gather into barns: yet your heavenly Father feedeth them. Are ye not much better than they?" I don't know if were better or not, but I know He was right there with me. He provided us with all the wonderful gifts we needed. We had our red Western Flyer wagon, we had coal for our stove, and we had shelter and food. We had each other, we had a Father in Heaven. What a wonderful coincidence.

We would take our wagon about a mile and a half to a large grocery store and get what groceries we needed, including a $3.00 dollar hundred pound bag of potatoes. That wagon hauled just about everything. Potatoes were one of the cheapest things we could buy, $3.00 for one hundred pounds was cheap. So we ate a lot of potatoes. I learned and read and figured out a lot of new recipes for potatoes. We ate them fried, roasted, boiled, soup, mashed, you name it we ate it. We were pretty fond of macaroni and cheese as well. God saw to it that we never went hungry.

I had purchased a 22 caliber single shot rifle at Sears and Roebuck. I got to be a pretty good shot with it so we had our share of rabbit and squirrel. They were pretty good too the way Homer had taught me to cook them in the Dutch oven that he had given us. We made a stuffing from old bread and onions and roasted it all together. Homer also taught me how to clean and fry fish. Again I could go on and on about how we cooked and made our meals. Suffice to say we did well.

Chapter 8

There were a few very bad moments or incidents. I will never forget the horrible evening when our mother came in. She had run into Dick and he had told her where we were. She was as we used to say as drunk as a skunk. She had also brought a man with her, he was as drunk as she was. They were pawing at each other and then went into Molly's room where they spent the night. I was in; I guess you could call it, a state of total confusion. I didn't know what to do. All I knew was that this was not good. Very early the next morning the man got up and started to bother Molly. I told him "leave her alone" but he just knocked me down and laughed at me and then started to take off her clothes. Molly was only 7 years old at the time and you could see the terror in her eyes and certainly hear it in her screams for help. It was obvious to me that he had every intention of raping her. I yelled for our mother but she was still passed out in Molly's bed. Molly was screaming for help and then I remembered my rifle.

I picked up my rifle and loaded a bullet into it… I then pointed it at the man and screamed at him. "Get out, get out of here or I'll shoot you". He looked at me and just laughed. The next thing I knew he was getting up and coming towards me. I again yelled "stop or I'll shoot you". "You won't shoot me, you're too scared" he said and started towards me again. I pulled the trigger. There was dead silence for a long second except for Molly's crying. The bullet did not fire. I watched as the man began to regain his composer. Meanwhile I quickly reloaded the rifle. He again laughed but he had stopped coming towards me. His laugh was a lot shallower than before as he said:" I'm going to come and take that rifle from you and I'm going to"; and then he went into a little detail about where he would put it.

Before he could take another step towards me I said very loudly," I pulled the trigger once do you think I won't do it again? Just take one more step and find out. If you're not out of here by the time I count to 3, I will shoot you". He thought for a moment, but when I put the rifle to my shoulder and started to count, he ran out. Can you imagine what would have happened if I had shot him? It would have been the end of us being together for sure and I don't know what they would have done to me. I have no doubt that God had control of the whole situation. What a coincidence.

In the meantime I guess all of the noise had finally woke our mother up. She asked us "what's all the noise about what's going on?" Molly started yelling at her; "your boyfriend was going to hurt me and you didn't even care. Frank made him stop", she said. "I hate you, I hate you", she screamed over and over again. Mom never made a move towards Molly to comfort her. I just stood there and looked at the mess we called Mom, and then I said to her, "we want you to just get out of here and never come back. We don't need you anymore for anything ever again". I remember those words so well because later in my life they bothered me a lot, but at the time I meant them. She never even protested she just got up and left. None of us saw her again for many years. It was the last time I saw her for 15 years.

Shortly after that, Dick started not coming home a lot. He never told me where he went. I found out years later that he had gotten involved with a homosexual man and was used by him a great deal. When I did find out it became and still is one of my saddest memories. I don't know if I could have done anything to stop it but if I had known I would have tried

Chapter 9

It wasn't long after I turned eleven years of age that we were found out. Somehow one of our teachers had picked up on something we said or did and had put two and two together and had called the police. It was a horrible scene for me and the kids. I tried in vain to tell the police that we were fine but obviously they knew we were not. Molly was crying and begging me to help and I could not. I had tried to physically grab her and Billy so they had put me in handcuffs I could only watch as they put Molly into a police car and drove away. I don't think that it is possible for me to ever be more devastated than I was at that moment.

Billy and I were put into another car where we were taken to the regular city jail and put into a cell. I remember thinking, at least Billy and I were together. Billy was a very mature 5 year old by this time. We sat in that jail cell and devised what we thought was a good plan. It wasn't a good plan, but we thought it was. I said "Billy, if we could escape from here and go to Chicago and find one of dad's brothers or sisters, maybe they would help us". We had always heard that he had at least 10 brothers and sisters. We devised a plan so that we could escape from the jail. You know what? It worked, we did escape and we headed for Chicago.

It was winter and it was cold. It took us almost five days to get there. How was our Father in Heaven looking out for us? After 2 days and nights on the trip we were very hungry and awfully close to freezing to death, when a small town constable saw us. He picked us up and carried us to his home where his wife fed us and treated us like the little kids we were. He knew we were runaways. He certainly had no plans of releasing us but he was content to get us fed and rested before he turned us over to the state police. We were still desperate so as soon as they were asleep that night we quietly snuck out and headed for Chicago again. There is no doubt in my mind today that we would not have made it thru another night if it had not been for that wonderful couple. What a coincidence.

It was 180 miles from Davenport to Chicago, but we made it. I know that neither one of us thought about how big Chicago was. We had no idea of an address for any aunt or uncle. If we had an address we probably would not have been able to find it. We thought maybe we could look them up in the phone book. I know now how silly our plan was. I also know how desperate we felt. We had to try something.

The term Windy City is certainly true. You would have had no trouble in convincing either one of us that night. We tried to get some sleep and get warn in a parked car. We had brought a blanket from the constable's house, but it wasn't enough it was just too cold. As we were passing a large building that turned out to be the Randolph Street IC Station, we saw that there were benches inside and of course it was warm, and they had rest rooms. We thought of sleeping there when we saw a policeman looking at us. He of course spotted right away that we had no adult with us and became suspicious. In just a few minutes he had us in custody. We were just too tired, cold and beat up to even try to run.

We were taken to a Juvenile facility where Billy was taken away from me. This was another one of those moments in time that I will never forget. Billy and I begged them to keep us together, but to no avail. It was like living over again what I had been through with Molly. I know it must have been even worse for Billy. I did not see Billy again until many years later. He was the first of my brothers and sisters that I reconnected with though, 14 years later

From Chicago I was taken back to Davenport. A few days later I was taken before a juvenile judge. He said that, in his opinion, because of what I had done, including escaping from the jail in Davenport and going to Chicago, I was indeed a juvenile delinquent. He then sent me to a reform school in Eldora Iowa.

After I had been there for a few days I managed to run away again. No one seemed to understand. All I wanted was to find my brothers and sister and go somewhere where we could live in peace as a family, that was never going to happen. After a very cold night and day they found me hiding

Chapter 9

in a corn field and brought me back to the reform school. Needless to say, they were not too happy with me.

I was put into solitary confinement. The only thing I had to eat was bread and milk. I don't know exactly how long I was in solitary. All that I was allowed to have in that cell was a metal cot with a thin mattress on it, no blanket and there was a toilet in the corner. They did however, let me keep my little New Testament Bible from the Salvation Army. I was in that cell long enough that I was able to read through it at almost 2 times. I would absolutely have flipped out in solitary if I had not had that New Testament to read. I'll tell you now, I do know some things about torture, and solitary confinement is one of the worst. In that loneliness it makes you feel like no one cares or wants you, that you are a truly worthless piece of trash. But because of that Bible I knew my Father in Heaven was with me, I wasn't alone.

Chapter 10

I don't know how they found out about my situation, but some of my cousins, who lived in Waycross Georgia, Jim and Lorraine Caswell, did find out and had decided that Jim would drive up to Eldora and if everything worked out, get me and bring me back to their home. I would however have to agree to a few terms. Dr. Caswell, (Jim), drove all the way from Waycross to Eldora, made all the legal arrangements and then came to see me. He was at least a bit upset when he found out that I had been kept in solitary confinement.

    I had met him once long ago. As we sat and talked he explained what he was willing to do. He also said that he knew I had tried to run away a few times and that this would not be tolerated if I decided to come stay with them. He explained to me that Molly and Billy were in foster homes and that they were ok and that I had to accept this. If I would agree to these rules then they would be glad to have me come live with them. He said he knew that we could work everything out. Somehow in my heart I knew that I could trust him completely, He was the first adult I had met in my life that I felt that I could open up to, talk to, and he would understand. So I agreed and in two days I was on my way to Georgia.

    Lorraine and Jim were so good to me. When I arrived in Waycross I met there little boy Thomas (Tommy) age 3 and their baby girl Margaret (Maggie). Loraine was pregnant with a little boy whose name would be Johnathon (John Boy). Later on they would have a baby girl named Tammy.

    During the seven years I lived with them I was treated as one of the family by everyone. Tommy, Maggie, and John Boy became like my little brothers and sister. I'm sure that there were some psychological reasons that I took so easily to them. Tammy was born so close to the time that I left that I hardly got to know her or for her to know me. It was so easy to come to love them all so much. One day Jim took me aside and very seriously asked me if I would like to be adopted by them. I thought about it and for some reason I decided not to. I do regret that decision for a lot of reason, but that was the one I made.

Jim was the Okefenokee area counselor for the Boy Scouts. I went with them a few times and decided to join. It was some of my best memories in Waycross. I became an explorer and an Eagle Scout. In Waycross I had a great and normal life. There could not be a better place to grow up in, but for some silly reason I got it in my head that I had to be a substantial financial burden on Jim and Lorraine. I thought that the best thing I could do for them, because I loved them so much, was to relieve them of that burden. I also decided that I would do it as soon as I could.

Chapter 11

What did I do? As soon as I turned 18 I joined the Army. I did not realize it at the time but I still was trying to prove to myself that I was worth something. So when I joined the Army I joined the toughest unit they had. Airborne Rangers. All of the things in my life had to be somehow fixed. I was haunted by memories, memories like our parents leaving us, or solitary confinement. I needed to know that I was worth something, so by golly I was going to prove it. I was going to be one of the toughest soldiers there was. I was going to show the whole world. I found out how silly I was later on in life, but back then I was determined to make it through the training, it liked to have killed me, but I made it. I do not at this time want to go into my life in the United States Army. Perhaps another book at another time. If I do I will call it fiction because it would be hard for a lot of people to believe. So let's just move on.

During my last year in the Army I asked my childhood sweetheart, Miss Mary Morgan to be my wife. She said "yes", we were married in Hialeah Florida on June 16, 1962. When I was discharged from the Army that November, we moved from Columbus Georgia to Hialeah where her parents, John and Florence Morgan, lived. They were two wonderful people. Mary was the most wonderful mother and wife a man could possibly need or want. She was my partner then and always was until the day she passed away.

I didn't waste any time getting a job. I grabbed the first one to come along only two days after I arrived in Hialeah. It was working for Dade Paper Company doing all sorts of odd jobs for them. I cleaned presses, cut paper, swept the floors, whatever they asked I did. I knew it wasn't the job that I would keep all my life, so I kept my eyes and ears open for whatever else might come along.

Sure enough, on the way to and from work every day I passed a small fiberglass boat company, Seabird Boats. Every once in a while they would have one of the boats out front on a trailer. They were, in my eyes, very beautiful boats, twenty three feet long and gorgeous.

One day on the way home from work I stopped to look at one. A man asked me if there was anything he could do for me and I answered. Half-jokingly, "yes give me a job working here," the next thing you know I was working for Seabird boats. They were a small company then and they did everything by hand, including lay up the fiberglass hulls and decks. I really enjoyed that job. Very soon I had the job of supervisor of the trim department. We did all of the upholstering for seats and rails, put on all of the hardware, and if a customer wanted a galley or anything else we built it for them. It wasn't very long before business got so good that they had to build a new much larger factory to handle the orders.

While I was working for Seabird Mary and I purchased a home in Hialeah. A small 3 bedroom one bath home. It turned out we would need it. On January 30, 1964 we had a beautiful baby girl. We named her Tina. What a blessing she was. I finally had a child of my own.

I really enjoyed working for Seabird. I learned a great deal from the plant manager, Art. He also paid me to come to his home and work with him. He was a for sure boat person. At his home he did repairs on people's boats and, he also built and sold small race boats. The race boats were all made by hand using teak wood and oak. We never put a nail or screw into one of these boats. It was all tung and grove and wooden pegs. He was indeed an artist when it came to boats and I enjoyed so much learning from him. I actually got a good enough reputation that I was hired to help build part of a boat used in a James Bond movie.

I worked for Seabird for about three years, and Mary gave birth to our second child. Frank JR. was born with a serious problem. During her pregnancy Mary had come in contact with someone who had German measles. This caused my son to be born with his intestines outside of his body. The doctors said they thought it could be fixed and operated on Frank. He came through the first surgery with flying colors. After the surgery Frank looked so good, his skin color was beautiful, he was beautiful. He did have to stay at the hospital in an incubator for quite a while until he became

Chapter 11

stronger. Finally the doctors told us that he would be able to go home in 2 days. The very next day he had a relapse. They took him back into surgery but three days later he died. We never got to bring Frank home.

I have heard a lot of stories about parents who have lost a child. Some of them after several years. Some children die at birth. I want to set the record straight. I don't care how old or how long. The pain is just as bad. Mary and I were absolutely devastated. Thank God for Tina. Having her there after all that had happened was a true blessing. Thank you Lord for being there with us. I do not know how anyone could go thru the loss of a child without God.

The hospital and doctor bills were astronomical. I was making a good living at Seabird, but not enough to pay all those bills as well. So I went looking for a way to make more money. I went to a friend of mine from the Army, whose father was a partner in a Ford dealership, he went to his father and asked his father if he could help me out. His father was wonderful. There was an opening in his used car department for a shift manager, if I wanted it I could have it. When the job was explained to me, how could I refuse? The way it worked was; when a used car was sold by anyone I got a percentage of the commission. If I sold a car I got the full commission. I did so well monetarily on this job that I was able to pay off all of the hospital and doctor bills, plus my everyday expenses in record time.

Also while I was working there Mary and I had another son. His name is Michael. Michael was healthy and beautiful. Michael was born on March 21, 1967. The first day of spring. He was a breath of spring for us. Through all of this did I mention? What a coincidence. Am so grateful that God led me to The Ford dealership. It was without doubt a gift from God.

Chapter 12

I had however always had an uncomfortable feeling deep down inside about the way I was taught to sell a car. The techniques they used, they called them the Hull Dobbs Method, left me feeling a little bit bad sometimes. So when I had paid off all of my bills and was ahead of the game so to speak. I started thinking about getting what I thought of as a real job.

Miami was without doubt a tourist town. So I thought, what kind of job you can get in a tourist town, one that is respected and pays well. My neighbor across the street worked for Eastern Airlines as a mechanic and did very well. Why not try the airlines. One day I asked for a longer lunch and drove to the airport. There was no fancy entrance way into Miami National Airport back in December of 1967. You just turned off of 8th Avenue into the airport. As you drove towards the terminal you passed the offices and the large hangers for different airlines. The first major airline was National, I turned into their parking lot. I followed the signs that guided you to the employment office, parked and went in. I was apprehensive as I didn't have the slightest idea of what I was going to encounter.

I went to the receptionist desk. She asked "are you looking for employment?" "Yes" I said. She said "if you'll have a seat right over there, as she pointed to some chairs, "someone will be right with you." I sat there for a very short time when a gentleman came out and introduced himself to me and asked me to come with him. We went into his office where he asked me, "So you're looking for a job with National Airlines?" I told him I was looking to change the job I had and if I could find a job that I thought I might like I was going to take it. I look back now and realize that I was certainly dressed well as I had on a nice sharkskin suit and tie. Normal dress for my job at the dealership. I'm quite sure that helped with what was about to happen.

He asked me if I had time to take a short test. I said "yes if it's not too long." He took me to another room with a desk and chair, took the test papers out of a cabinet, gave me some instructions and told me to bring them to him when I was done. The test was one of those IQ type tests. I had always had no problem with those types of test. I finished it in about ten minutes and carried in to him. He asked. "Done already?" "Yes" I said "it was pretty simple." He didn't say anything he took out an overlay to check the test results. When he had finished he asked "if you are hired would you mind taking the polygraph test as required." I told him "not at all."

He then asked me questions. "Where do you work now? Why did you want to change jobs?" normal interview questions... When he had finished he said "National would be glad to have you if you pass the polygraph test." Also there was another set of standard employment forms that I would have to sign and agree to all of the terms. I actually became a little nervous because things had went to well and I didn't want to jump into something I might regret. After all I did have a good job. I thought for just a second and then I asked. "This is not a part time or seasonal job is it? I know that right now we are in our peak tourist season and I do have a good job right now. I wouldn't want to quit my job for one that's only temporary". "No" he said "the jobs that we have open right now will be permanent full time jobs". "You said jobs, what exactly would I be doing"? "Well right now we have openings on the ramp and in the terminal. I believe you would certainly be more suited for the terminal. As it pays more and its inside where you will be well dressed clean and dry".

I laughed at the humor intended and agreed. He went on to explain what an airline agents job mostly entailed. In my mind I thought I would like the job so I asked. "If I took the job would it be ok to give a two week notice to my current job? "I don't want to leave them high and dry, they have been wonderful to me", "sure" he said. "When do you think you might be able to fill out the other papers and take the polygraph"? We got together on the dates and I thanked him and left. I went into a lot of detail on how I got hired at National Airlines because it became a big part of my life for the next 36 years

Chapter 12

Working for a major airline in a major airport was quite a challenge. I was up to it though, young and healthy, and everything went well. It was a big change from the car lot. I was eager to learn, I always have been and I know that it was appreciated by my supervisors and managers. In no time at all I was doing quite well.

I want to mention one incidence that in many ways changed part of my life. I will not go into any details regarding the results of this incident in this book. Perhaps another book or another time. However, leading up to that incident, I was hired in January of 1968 and was as I said always eager to learn. I quickly saw that one of the positions everyone but a very few shied away from was international ticketing. I always loved a challenge so I asked around a little on how I might get a chance to learn international ticketing. The supervisor who always bid the midnight shift told me. "If you will bid midnights, which are always open for bid, I will teach you. Most all of our complicated international problems come to us on that shift due to the fact that the agents in the north, mostly Kennedy airport don't like, or don't know how, to do the job. So they put the passengers who are making international connections on the flight to Miami and tell them to go to our ticket counter there and we will fix their tickets. Nice aren't they"?

Well I bid the midnight shift and I did learn. I also learned how to fix problems with most of the South American carriers. We kept a very large stock of Taylor Champagne at the airport. Most of the time those foreign carriers would be oversold. We always seemed to have a connecting passenger or two that didn't get booked correctly in New York. A bottle or two of Taylor's got them a seat on their flight.

While I was working the night shift, August 4, 1968, I was asked to meet what we called an extra section out on the International concourse. I was told that it required someone with a security clearance. I didn't even know until then that they had checked out my Army background and I had been given a high security clearance, so I went to meet the flight.

It turned out that the flight I was to meet had been chartered by The Richard Nixon Campaign to use while he was running for president. He was arriving in Miami for the Republican National Convention on Miami Beach. There were some strange circumstances at the gate but, maybe another book or another time. After meeting the flight we were in the process of navigating our way through the several security gates that were on the international concourse, this gave me an opportunity to talk with him. One of the results from our conversation was, that I got invited to come to the convention on Miami Beach, if I wanted to. I chose to come the last night. It was fun and somewhat exciting as that was the night he was nominated. The result of this coincidental meeting caused a lot of changes in my life. However, another book or another time.

I must have been doing a good job for the airline because about one year later I was asked, much to the chagrin of some of my much more senior fellow workers, to take on the job of vacation relief supervisor. We had a strong union. It was a closed shop so I had to join. Unions were never my thing. Most everything was done according to seniority not necessarily qualifications. However when it came to part time positions the management had the right to choose whom they may. They asked me. I knew it would upset a few of the "old timers" but it was too good of an opportunity for me including the additional money I would get as a supervisor It didn't take long for most of them to get over it. One day one of them approached me and said. "We were mad at first that they had picked you for the job but we are glad now because you are fair and you help a lot. You're a really hard worker." I will always treasure that.

In the meantime I was asked to take on some additional responsibilities as well. I was asked to work with the tour operators. The reason they used was partly because I had picked up ticketing so well and group travel required different types of tickets. Perhaps one day I will be able to explain the other reasons. This worked out rather well because I was able to go to places like New Orleans and Las Vegas and all of our overseas destinations to help handle some of the problems that had occurred, also the tour companies seemed to like me. I also got to work at the airport with the Miami Dolphins. They are still my favorite team.

Chapter 13

We lived in Hialeah Florida for eight years when we began to feel a little cramped in our small home. Our children were growing up and with four of us, one bathroom was not a good thing. We decided to sell our home and look for another larger home. We made out very well on the sale and we were able to purchase a very nice new 3 bedroom two bath home in south Miami. Our new home was only 5 miles above the Florida Keys. All of us liked salt water fishing quite a bit, so being this close to the Keys was wonderful. In the eight years we lived in South Miami we fished the Keys a lot. If you enjoy fishing you would love the Keys. Make sure you have good fishing gear because when you fish in or near the Gulf Stream there is no telling what you might catch, a forty or fifty pound fish was not rare. One day while fishing on the (what they call) flats in the upper keys, Tina caught a large trout. She was pretty good about handling fish but this was her first trout and it bothered her because it was so soft to touch. "Will you take this off the hook for me," she asked, "sure" I answered, "let me set my rod down and I'll get it for you." I had just purchased a new Garcia Mitchell 300 rod and reel; I laid it down and reached to get her trout off of the hook; the last I saw of my new rod and reel was a trail of churned up bottom flying away from our boat. A barracuda had grabbed my bait and the rest was history. I guess you could say "lesson learned". My family thought it was funny. Eventually, they even made me laugh about it.

While our children were growing up in south Florida, there were many happy years and events. One of our neighbors was the field goal kicker for the Miami Dolphins, his wife taught my children in the elementary school just down the street. In my yard was a big avocado tree. My kids would load up their wagon and sell them to neighbors, the neighbors loved them and bought them all. That was nice because it gave my kids a feeling of independence on how to make spending money for themselves. So you can see that some of our best memories were in South Florida.

South Florida has what I call perfect weather, except for the occasional hurricane. During the 16 years we lived in the Miami area we experienced at least 6 Hurricanes. The worst one for us hit while we still lived in Hialeah. The hurricanes name was Cleo. Cleo's wind speed was measured at 130 miles per hour while it was still way off the coast, then the winds from the storm blew the wind speed gauge off of the hurricane storm center in Miami, As far as we know the true top speed is unknown. Cleo's eye came directly over where we lived in Hialeah. The wind blew so hard that it forced water between the CBS blocks of our home and ruined the carpets. I remember a coconut that came thru the plywood I had put over the windows in one of the bedrooms. Coconuts become cannon balls in a hurricane. The worst part of a hurricane is the aftermath. After Cleo we were unable to even drive around for several days because of the debris and we were without water and power for about 12 days. Hurricanes however, are quickly forgotten because of the almost year round wonderful weather. I miss that wonderful weather, and the fishing at this very moment.

Chapter 14

Later on Mary wanted to move to Orlando Florida. Her Mom and Dad had moved there and she wanted to be near them. She had always been close to her family. I put in a transfer request and it didn't take long before, for several reasons, it was approved. National Airlines had, because of deregulation in the airline industry, started flying international routes. They flew to London, Paris, Amsterdam and Frankfurt to start. I had become recognized as one of the best international agents they had and was given the job of working with customs and immigrations. I took care of documents and such. Coincidently, they were at the time I asked to transfer, planning to start nonstop flights to Europe out of Orlando, just to London and Paris at first. Since everything in Miami was well set up they were glad to have me go to Orlando to help set up the procedures there.

Just before all of this could take place we merged with Pan American Airways. There had always been a partnership of one kind or the other between Pan Am and National. For instance the first airline to fly Jet aircraft in the United States was National Airlines. That came about because of an agreement between National and Pan Am. Pan Am owned a fleet of 707 jets, no one else had jets at that time. Pan Am would fly into the USA at either Los Angeles, Miami or New York and then National would fly the aircraft from there to a Pan Am departure city. At that time because of regulations Pan Am could not have a route to fly inside the 48 States.

When we became merged there was quite a bit of shuffling going on. After a while I was, so to speak, loaned out to a company called SATO, Scheduled Airlines Traffic Office. I was still a Pan Am employee. Each

American owned airline owned one share of SATO and each agent was handpicked by a committee to work at Sato. There were some different reasons that I was moved to Sato, but I wish to save them for another book or another time. What Sato mainly did was arrange all travel for the government and all branches of the military. They had over three hundred offices around the world. They were originally formed during World War Two and for security reasons, awarded Anti-Trust immunity. I would like to input one thought at this point. I worked as a Sato employee for twenty of my years at National Pan Am. I am proud of everything that I did and I believe that I did them all well.

SATO was and still is a great organization. I was given the title of Branch Manager Two, which means I had more than one office to handle. I was also picked to work as a trouble shooter when another office had problems anywhere in the world. As you can imagine I traveled a lot. I consider a lot of my travel a blessing. To be able to go and see so many different countries and cities was wonderful. I would never have thought as a little boy sitting in a shack on the Mississippi River in Davenport Iowa, that I would ever be able to do any of this.

I was able to take Mary along with me on many occasions. She traveled like a trouper. I found out years later that she was what you call a white knuckle traveler. She was scared to fly and never mentioned it to me. My children Michael and Tina were able to travel a lot as well. For instance Tina was able to go to Hawaii with a friend of hers as a graduation present to both of them. By the way they really milked it and got two weeks in Hawaii. On a trip to Europe they once were treated to a very private and wonderful tour of a part of Germany that most people do not get to see. A friend of mine Helmut Gouch in a town called Traub-Traubach took them on the tour. He had put on his lederhosen and was absolutely wonderful.

I won't, as I mentioned earlier go into some of the details of my travel. But there are couple of fun trips I would love to tell you about.

I had always felt a great deal of love and gratitude in my heart for my cousins, Jim and Lorraine. I had tried many times to get the airlines to give them passes. I thought it only right since they had taken me in for so long and had indeed been my legal guardians. Finally the airline gave in. After that I could take them anywhere Pan American flew. I was able to take them First class on a month long trip to Europe. By the way Jim was 6 feet

Chapter 14

6 inches tall and being able to have first class seats for him was great. We flew into London, drove to Scotland and back to London the first week and a half. Then we flew from London to Hamburg Germany, drove from Hamburg to Amsterdam via the Northern route over the Great Dyke, then we drove to Paris via Luxemburg, Belgium and down the Mosel River valley. Jim and I both loved to paint in oils and acrylics so we made a point of visiting all of the great museums in route, Mary and Lorraine shopped.

In Scotland we visited a lot of spots that were in the Caswell family history. For instance, one of our ancestors had been Bishop Caswell who was Bishop of the Isles and lived in a castle in Oban Scotland called Carnasserie Castle. We went to the castle and also to the cemetery where he was buried. He had been buried next to a relative of his, King Bruce. A wonderful old gentleman who was grounds keeper at the cemetery was thrilled to show us around when he found out we were kin to the Bishop. We had an absolutely wonderful trip and I was thrilled that I could provide it for them and us. I wasn't quite done yet I had a few other ideas but I had to find out what else they would like to see or do.

Jim told me on the way back home from Europe, that one day he would like to go to Washington, our nation's capital. I knew I could manage that so I started making plans. I asked him if we went what would be at the top of his list of things to see. He told me that there was an art exhibit at the National Museum. It was a collection of paintings from stately homes and castles in England. Then he said he had always wanted to visit the White House. He also named several other things he would like to do time permitting. We got together and set up our days and times. Their son Thomas was a Chiropractor as was Jim, and was working in Jim's Chiropractic office. He was happy for his mom and dad's opportunity to travel and agreed again to take care of Jim's patents for him in his absence. I told you he was a great kid.

We flew to Washington picked up a rental car and began our sightseeing. We went to the home of George Washington in Virginia. We spent a day in the Smithsonian. On the third day we went to my congressman's office and got passes for the White house. That afternoon we went to the White house. The congressional pass was a little better than getting in line at the White house and being led in the side door and out the front door. You got to see a few more rooms and had a little better guide service. Jim was happy, that was something he had always wanted to do.

What a Coincidence

The next day however I had a big surprise for him. I wouldn't tell him what it was. All I told him was, we need to dress up, I'm talking suits and ties and that the ladies had to wear nice dresses. I had not even told Mary where we were going. We ate a small breakfast and I called a cab. I quietly told the cab driver where to go. When we pulled up to the back gate at the White House Jim asked. "Isn't this the White House?" "Yes" I said. "We were here yesterday. Why are we back?" He asked. "Let's just go see" I said. I gave the guard at the gate a slip of paper that I had and he called for a golf cart to come and get us. We were driven to the back of the White House where bleachers had been set up and several people had already began to gather. We were led into a roped off area right next to a large podium. Just about then they announced over the speaker "Ladies and Gentlemen, distinguished guests, the President of the United States Ronald Reagan and Mrs. Reagan also the President of Ecuador Febres Cordero and Mrs. Cordero." President Reagan came to the podium with several other people with the playing of Hail to the Chief. With them was the Vice President, the Secretary of State and several other dignitaries. They played the National Anthem of both countries and then with a 105 howitzer battery fired a 21 gun salute. Both President Reagan and the President of Ecuador Febres Cordero made a short speech. Probably because it was cold outside. And then we went inside. Jim as I said, was 6'6" tall and he stood out well with his mouth open and in awe.

We were then asked to come in to the blue room where a reception was being held for the President of Ecuador. Jim, Lorraine and Mary were absolutely in some kind of trance, I know that they were amazed, Remember, my job was to provide travel for government employs and military personnel. So suffice to say I knew someone who knew someone that made this possible. I can't begin to tell you how good it made me feel to be able to do this for Jim and Lorraine. I know that neither one of them will ever forget that White House visit. What a coincidence.

Chapter 15

In the meantime Mary had decided that she wanted to do something with her life. She had always had a green thumb and loved flowers so she registered for a floral school at one of the local colleges.

When she graduated she had no trouble getting a job in a florist shop as a designer. She worked for a very sweet lady for over a year when she approached me with the idea that she would like to have her own shop. She was so happy in this work. How could I refuse? We rented a store in a new strip mall in a great location and I built her a shop inside. It turned out real nice and it was large because we had rented two sections.

She ran that store for over eight years and we actually open a second store across from The University of Central Florida. I believe those were some of her happiest years. The stores were called Southern Elegance I and II. She made each of them beautiful because of her wonderful talents. I was always relegated to things like delivery, or striping thorns off of roses, or during certain holidays I could arrange a dozen roses or make a corsage. My son Michael's first job was driving the delivery van. Tina was always a very good designer and helped a great deal when needed. I remember one, now funny, incident. I was at work some twenty miles away, when I got a phone call from Mary, she was in a panic. Her and her designers were up on the designers table because a snake had come into the shop. They had been spraying some flowers by the back door and the snake had come in. She was yelling at me on the phone to do something. I quickly asked her what the snake looked like, from her description it was a very long black snake. At least I knew it was not poisonous. I then reminded her that I was twenty miles away and that I thought she should call the fire department or police. About that time her mailman came into the store and asked what in the world was going on. When he was told he went to where the snake had crawled under a shelf, reached in and pulled the snake out. It was a very big Blue Indigo snake, the postman's brother ran the reptile exhibit at the Sanford zoo so he called him to come and get the snake. To my knowledge that snake is still in the zoo.

Mary and I had joined a small Independent Baptist Church. Mary always had a soft spot for the kids. Guess what so did I, When you go back to the beginning of this book you can see why my heart was there. Mary's love for children was I truly believe, greater than mine. We often prayed and asked God what He wanted us to do. The idea of a children's church came into our hearts. Should we or shouldn't we? We believed the answer was yes. We went to our pastor and asked him if we could work with the children in some capacity. Perhaps a Children's Church. He thought it was a great idea. So we started a service for the children during the same time as what we called the big church. I'm sure we fumbled around some but we enjoyed what we were doing and so did the children.

One Wednesday night in church the pastor shared some information with the church. He said the First Baptist Church in Hammond Indiana, Pastor Jack Hyles, was having another Pastors Conference. He had held these before with a terrific turnout. What our pastor was asking was if at all possible he would like to attend.

Our little church didn't have a lot of money for extra activities like this, But, Right away I realized I could help if he and the church would be willing. I had the capability to obtain a free rental car for him to use. He then would only need the gas money. Our church was the sending church for a missionary in Mexico that had said he would like to attend as well. He could come to Orlando and help with the drive to Hammond and help with the gas.

I did throw in one stipulation. I wanted to go as well. I could not drive up with them at the time they needed to go, but I could fly up on the second day of the weeklong conference and then drive back with them. I could also help share the motel and gas bills. This was all agreed upon. I don't know what made me want to go but something was pushing me. Well I got the car for them and they took off for Indiana. My trip up to Hammond turned out somewhat strange.

Chapter 15

I could pick and choose the flights I wanted. For some reason, I'm sure it had to do with my schedule, I chose to go on Continental with a connection in Indianapolis. I hated connections but that's what I chose. When we arrived in Indianapolis our connecting flight developed a mechanical problem. That's why I did not like connections. That meant we would arrive at Chicago's O'Hare Airport about two hours late. The church was picking people up at the airport and driving them to the church. You were required to give them your flight and arrival times.

I had been unable to get hold of anyone to let them know about our delay so I expected I would have to use plan B, I would be on my own. This didn't bother me a lot as I was indeed a very capable traveler. I would make sure that no one was there to pick me up. Then I would hurry down to the shuttle bus that ran from O'Hare Airport to Midway Airport and from there catch a cab to Hammond. Troublesome but simple.

When our flight landed at O'Hare I was the first one off the flight and down the concourse in a flash. I asked at the passenger service counter if I had any messages and I checked again in the baggage claim area. No messages. I took off to the other end of the airport for the shuttle terminal.

When I arrived at the shuttle station, I was what you would consider lucky, the shuttle was just ready to leave. Just as I was ready to step into the shuttle I heard a buzzing sound from a far distance page. There is no way you could understand it, but it stopped me cold. The driver asked if I was going or not. I thought for just a second and said, "thank you but not."

Somehow I knew that it was my name on that page. I hurried back to Continental Airlines and sure enough a van driver from the church had been paging me. It seems I had moved to fast for him to catch me when I had gotten off the flight.

I have ridden in cabs in Tokyo Japan. If you ever have then you know what I am trying to say here. This van driver had obviously trained in Tokyo, I know we made it to the church in record time. As we pulled up to the church it was the first time I had realized how big First Baptist Church of Hammond was. The foyer ran the length of one block with several doors and even wrapped around the corner. The driver asked me if there was any special spot I wanted to be dropped. I told him anywhere, in the middle would be good.

I went in having no idea at all on how I would go about finding my friends. At that moment a man approached me and asked "You're Mr.

Tracy, aren't you?" "Yes" I replied, somewhat stunned by the fact that he had called me by name. The foyer was full of people and I certainly didn't have a name tag. What happened next, happened so fast I didn't have time to ask how he knew my name. "The services have started" he said "so please follow me and I'll take you to your friends." He led me up to the top balcony and to an empty seat next to my pastor and friend. I think all three of us were amazed that I had found them. Just as I was sitting down a pastor from California began to preach. His message was on the importance of reaching Gods favorites, His children. Suffice to say, I would not have made it in time to hear this message if, I had not heard the page at the airport, if I had not had a Tokyo cab driver and if that gentleman had not led me up to my friends. What a bunch of coincidences.

The speaker centered his message on his son who had Cerebral Palsy. The way that he presented the message touched my heart. When he gave an invitation, and a challenge; I made my way to the alter. It took me quite a while but I made it. When I arrived there I got on my knees and promised God that I would work with children, teaching them about God and More importantly how to get to Heaven. I have been trying my very best to keep that promise. Sometimes I feel as if I have fallen short. But God has blessed me with the many times when I have felt really good about everything. When we arrived back in Orlando I was on fire. I couldn't wait to get going full blast. I wanted to reach so many more children. We started out strong with visitation. And the attendance grew.

Chapter 16

Mary and I had never had a real wedding. We had been married by a Justice of the Peace in Hialeah Florida. So I wanted to do something special for her. Our twenty sixth wedding anniversary was coming up, our twenty fifth had sort of slipped by. As secretly as possible I got together with the church and the ladies in the church so that we could have a ceremony and redo our vows. At the flower shop I arranged for Mary's head designer to make up flowers for a full-fledged wedding, Candelabra, arches, everything. Our wedding anniversary fell on a Wednesday so it was set it up for Wednesday night service at the church. I had invited her relatives from all over to come. I want you to know it totally surprised her. When she came into the church that evening and "Here Comes the Bride" started playing, all she could do was giggle a funny giggle with tears running down her cheek. All of the relatives showed up, and the ladies in the church had prepared a fantastic feast for after the service. All I can say is, it was wonderful.

A short time later we learned a valuable lesson. There is such a thing as politics in a church. I won't say anything more about that. However we felt hampered. Things were not going as we had planned. But do you know what? We did not get discouraged. God, beyond any doubt, put in our hearts that we were not where He wanted us. We prayed very hard for help. In our hearts we knew that we had to move on to another church.

We had visited another small Missionary Baptist church on occasion. They very often had Gospel music singers there and Mary and I both enjoyed good Gospel music. Also I believe that both of us were impressed with their way of worship. So we started attending services there.

We were there for a short time when God laid it on our hearts to ask "if we became members, would we be able to work with the children." The Pastor responded by saying. "We thought you would never ask. We would love to have you both." We met with the pastor over lunch after church and before lunch was over we had another youth church. What a coincidence.

When we accepted the challenge. There were only eleven children in the church so we had work to do and we welcomed it. The church had a separate small building that they used for a fellowship hall. They allowed us to turn it into a children's church on Sundays and we also used it for special occasions for the children, such as an Easter egg hunt etc. It was perfect.

The first Sunday we held children's church I asked the children to set up their eleven chairs in one row across the front. I taught them a lesson that Sunday about prayer, on how to pray and the power of prayer. At the end of the service I gave an invitation, reminding them of Gods promises in regards to prayer. At the end of the invitation I asked them," would you like to pray for our children's church to grow, and maybe for a bus or a van, if so please just stand up, turn around and kneel down and use the chairs as an altar." All eleven of them responded.

It was just two days later that we received the phone call. Orlando is a large city. Especially in size. It is at least 50 miles across in each direction. A church over 50 miles away, way over on the other side of town, called us out of the blue. There reason was that they had two busses that they were not going to use any more and would we be interested in one or both of them? At Wednesday night service I addressed the church on what had transpired and asked if the church would be ok if we took one of the busses, if it was in good working order? Their response was yes.

One of our members was a mechanic and went with me Thursday. We picked out what he said he thought was the best bus and drove it back to our church, these were the days before CDL licenses were required to drive a bus. All I want to say now is WOW. In less than a month we found out you could put 70 small children on a 45 passenger bus. I have one question. Do you believe that God answered the prayers of those eleven children? Or, was it just a coincidence?

Mary and I were the leaders of the youth ministry at that church for ten years. During that time we saw many of what we truly believe were

Chapter 16

miracles. After we had the junior church going we thought of Vacation Bible School. I went to the senior Deacon and the pastor and asked;" How long has it been since you held a Vacation Bible School?" They had to think for a long time and then the senior Deacon said; "I believe that it's been over 30 years." "I was wondering" I said, "if we might possibly have one now?" The senior deacon responded with "Well I suppose it would depend on a lot of things, like what would it cost?" I know that the Holy Spirit was answering questions for me because without thinking I said; "about five hundred dollars." "Well we could manage that. How many kids do you think we would have?" Again without thinking I answered; "about two hundred." They laughed and said, "Well that would be wonderful but that's a lot of kids." (BY the way, we had two hundred and twenty two kids attend our VBS) "Well when would we hold it?" The pastor asked. "As soon as we can after school lets out," I answered. Then the pastor said, "Well if you want to get started on it go ahead, but let's don't make any definite plans. Let's see how it goes at first." I told them that that would be fine. Somehow in my heart I knew we were going to have Vacation Bible School.

Everything moved along wonderfully well. In no time at all we had enough volunteers. To save money and to involve all ages in the process, I asked the more elderly ladies if they would bake snacks for the kids. We could have cookies on Monday, Cupcakes on Tuesday, etc. On Wednesday night we would have a Family Fun Night. We would forgo crafts that night and have one service with everyone together, the children and their families. After the service have hotdogs, hamburgers, chips, drinks and something for desert. WE did have to spend some money on crafts but even there God provided. Hobby lobby gave us a lot of pieces left over from when they made mats for picture frames. We used them to make small picture frames for one of our crafts. Everyone thought we had a great plan.

My mind went to what I would do or who could I get to do a service for the Family Fun Night. I prayed a great deal about it because the word clown kept popping up in my mind. I didn't know anything about clowns and I wasn't sure where that was coming from. I finally gave in. It had to be from God. I called all of the clown phone numbers in the phone book, but to no avail. When I talked to some of them, the language they used I wouldn't want them around our kids. Others, when I mentioned two hundred kids (well that's what Jesus told me) they wanted a fortune. I was

What a Coincidence

beginning to think that I had misunderstood what God wanted. It was less than three weeks before VBS and I still didn't have a clown.

I was driving East on hi way 50 in Orlando with Mary when I realized what my problem was. I had been trying to find a clown, I. I began praying as I was driving. "Dear Lord forgive me. I need your help. If you do want a clown at our Vacation Bible School then I am turning it over to you. Please forgive me for not trusting you and thinking I could do it myself. Amen. I turned to Mary, who by the way was looking at me a little funny, and asked. "Would you like to go on home and fix dinner, or would you rather stop up here at Denny's and get something?" That was one of the easiest sales I ever made. We went to Denny's. We went in and ordered. I don't remember what Mary ordered but I ordered one of those cholesterol bombs, country fried steak. The waiter brought our order and I believe I had taken two bites when in the front door of Denny's came two clowns. They were in complete beautiful costume. The hostess sat them at the table right next to us. What a coincidence.

I sat there and listened as they answered what would seem to be a very good question from the waiter. "Why are you in costume?" They explained that they had just left a church where they had just finished a show for the kids in that church. I was over to that table in a flash. I asked them if I could sit down for a minute and ask them a question. They answered "sure please have a seat" "Have you ever worked at a Vacation Bible School?" I asked. To make the story short those wonderful clowns not only came to our VBS but they brought five other Christian clowns with them. God had packed our church that night. We had put folding chairs in the aisles and still had standing room only, the clowns put on a show that explained the gospel so well a child could understand it. When they had finished their program, they turned the invitation over to the pastor and thirty two people came forward and asked the lord into their hearts.

After the service was over I helped the clowns clean up and put their equipment into their van. I was still amazed at how wonderfully well everything had gone. I had to ask. "What do you have to do to become a clown?" He answered." If you're really serious what you have to do is go to a clown college." I asked "where are they located." They told me, that "the best one was just south of Orlando in Sarasota Florida." I gathered all the information that I could before they left, thanking them over and over again.

Chapter 16

Those clowns and Mary and I became good friends over the next few years. Mary and I both ended up attending Clown College. Mary went right after I did when she saw how much fun it could be. We joined their clown alley and worked different Christian gigs with them all over Central Florida. We met the flights that brought the "Make a Wish" children to Orlando, we also worked Disney Worlds Facility for children with terminal cancer. There were so many wonderful organizations working with kids in need and I believe we went to them all. Mary's clown name was "Lavender Lou" and mine was "Puzzles."

As the next few years passed we spent just about all of our spare time sharing the Gospel of our Lord and Savior with children anywhere they would let us go. At the same time we never stopped working at our church. We felt as if we were right where God wanted us. Was all of this just a coincidence?

Chapter 17

One Sunday evening at church our pastor read a letter to the congregation. The letter had been sent to the church from an organization called Child Evangelism Fellowship (CEF). It was a letter inviting any born again Christian who wanted to, to attend a class called "Teaching Children Effectively 1" It was just as the name said, a method of teaching children effectively. It would require the student to attend once a week in the evening for 3 to 4 hours for 12 weeks. There was a one hundred dollar fee for materials. Much to our surprise the pastor said that he was familiar with CEF and that they were indeed a great organization and that the church would be glad to pay the cost if anyone was interested. So? He asked who would like to go. I believe that Mary's hand and mine went up the same time. Mary and I had been doing a lot of praying at that time because we felt that there was something missing in what we were doing. Oh the children were having a great time and they were learning a lot but, we felt that we were not doing a good job accomplishing our main goal, decisions for Christ. Could this be the answer?

Child Evangelism Fellowship became one of the most important things in our lives. We attended that class and we learned things that made everything so much clearer. WE learned how to teach children effectively. What we learned I know we will never forget. It was awesome.

I'll be the first one to admit that Mary was a much better student than me. Where I struggled she excelled. When we finished that course and took what we had learned back to our children's church, it was indeed like a miracle. Many children at our church began to understand so much more and came to know the Lord as Savior. We have since then always used CEF materials to teach with. They are so easy to use, so easy to understand and for the child's benefit so wonderfully illustrated. Every CEF lesson, memory verse, song and even their missionary stories, have the Gospel message linked into them. This gives every child an opportunity to accept Jesus as their own. How could it get any better?

After that we become involved in CEF work in the Central Florida area. We helped in the fair ministry, we volunteered to work at the Salvation Army's rescue mission. We also helped out in what they called Good News Clubs in different locations such as churches and government housing projects. Mary became a teacher and helper at one of the first public school Good News clubs in Orlando, or Florida. Union Park Elementary. Another wonderful lady named Mary had walked in front of this school for months, maybe more, praying that God would open the door there for a club. He did and it was awesome. Being able to reach children in the public schools, what a concept. I think we had fallen in love with CEF.

Because of our work with CEF we became familiar with their whole ministry. They were one of the world's largest children's ministries. At this time they were in all 50 states and over 150 countries. Their headquarters are in Warrenton Missouri. In Warrenton they have a college that taught a lot deeper course in teaching children. It was not cheap but it was not ridiculously high either. Mary and I again prayed a lot about possibly going there for the course. We were not spring chickens and the thought of going to school again was a serious consideration. There was also the time and the money that would be needed.

That course was also twelve weeks long but it was 5 long days a week and we were told it entailed a great many hours of homework. Because of my seniority with Pan Am I had accumulated well over two months' vacation time and because of what my job entailed I had more comp time coming than I could count. Mary's staff at the florist shops were quite able to handle things there. That took care of the time we needed. We knew that we would learn a great deal but we also knew that with the learning would come a much larger commitment. We decided to go. We flew into St Louis and were picked up by the school. Warrenton is about sixty miles due west of St. Louis.

I have attended classes in a lot of different circumstances. This one was different. We lived in a dormitory room at the facility and ate in a cafeteria there as well. The room was very adequate and the meals were great. This was all part of the fee. What was really different was the class time and the homework time. We started classes early in the Morning, 8:30AM to be exact. Brook for a one hour lunch. And back to class until 5: PM with a short 15 minute break in that period. There were no radios, no TVs allowed. We were very often up past midnight doing homework. The good part of that was the comradery we had with the other students. We were all, without exception glad to help one another. There were a lot of practicums and presentations to perform throughout the course. But we, with God's grace, made it through the course. By graduating we were now qualified to go home and teach others. We were indeed teachers. We were able to help CEF much more in Central Florida.

Somewhere in this story I need to mention that Pan American Airlines went Bankrupt. I found out while at work when it popped up on my computer. I wasn't too surprised because of everything that had taken place so far. I did however surprise my office staff by getting on my knees in the office and praying, "Thank you Lord for everything, I don't know exactly what will happen now but I know that you do, so thank you for whatever wonderful things you have planned for me. Amen." I had hardly gotten back in my chair when my private line rang. It was SATO headquarters calling to tell me "don't you go anywhere, we are picking up your employment and well get with you soon to go over the details." I lost some benefits, such as my retirement, but my pay stayed the same and I kept my seniority and I was able to start a 401K. I still had all the airline passes that I would or could need on any of the other carriers.

Chapter 18

Mary and I stayed very busy. Part of that staying busy was to see our daughter Tina married to a sailor who had just graduated from the Navy Nuclear Power School in Orlando a Mr. Bill Crawford. There were some doubts, after all no man is good enough for your daughter. Right after they were married they had to go to Saratoga Springs, New York. There was a nuclear training center there for Submarines. While they were there my beautiful granddaughter Victoria (Tori) was born. I will never forget that day for several reasons, my first grandchild for instance. Mary had to be there, Mary by the way had bought a stuffed bear so big it required a seat on the flight as well. I got her a pass to fly on US Airlines to Buffalo. Buffalo was about 50 miles from Saratoga Springs mostly Interstate and an easy drive, or so I thought. Mary's flight had no sooner left when I found out a blizzard like storm was going to hit that area? I knew that she was going to try and get there no matter what I said so I called the rental car company and had them change her car to a four wheel drive. She called me after Tori was born to let me know she had made it ok. That 4 wheel drive had gotten her through. She said a lot of other cars had slid off the interstate but she made it. Mary had never even seen a lot of snow, let alone drive in it, but you can't stop a determined Grandma.

Later on Tina and her family moved to Charleston South Carolina where my second beautiful granddaughter Veronica Nichole (NIKKI) was born. Bill was assigned to Boomer subs out of Charleston Navy yard.

I need to tell you about my wonderful son Michael don't I? Well he found a wonderful girl named Matilda. They were married and lived in Orlando. They still do. They have no children together but Matilda has a daughter, Shelly, from a previous marriage who now has two daughters of her own, Merry and Tylor. That gave me two Great granddaughters. I cannot even begin to brag enough about all of them. I man could in no way want a better son and Daughter-in-law.

Bill and Tina had moved to Groton Connecticut where he was still assigned to Boomer subs. While they were there Bill decided that he did not want to be married anymore so he managed an undesirable discharge from the Navy and abandoned Tina and the girls. The only way Mary and I could help was to go and get them and bring them back to live with us. They did for a total of 6 years. Then Tina found Victor Carini. They were married just before we moved to Georgia as missionaries. They now also have a beautiful son named Jacob as well as Tori and Nikki.

Tori now lives in New Jersey. Just across the river from New York City, where she works in the Roosevelt Hotel. From all I hear she is doing well as a New Yorker. Nikki is married to a good man who is in the Air force and stationed at Robins Air force base in Warner Robins Georgia as an air policeman. His name is Beau. They have one also beautiful little girl named Isabella (Bella). They have a baby boy on the way at the time of this writing.

I have my share of grandchildren and great grandchildren. I love them all a lot. I often wish I could see them more often but we all have our own lives to live, don't we?

Well a few more years passed. During that time we felt called to go to another church. We attended the new church for about a year and a half. We were staying so busy working with CEF that we avoided making very many commitments to the church. Believe me we stayed busy. Between our Christian clowning and our volunteer work with CEF we kept a full calendar

Chapter 19

Over the Years Mary and I had come to enjoy the change of seasons in the mountains of North Georgia. We had gone there in the fall every year for a long time. Over those years a very good friend of mine from the airlines had built a home in Hiawassee Georgia, right on Lake Hiawassee. Mary, the kids and I would often stay with them for a few days. It was one of those gifts from God that we really loved.

One year though we talked about maybe going to see the fall leaves somewhere else. Just for a change. Our fame as clowns and teachers had spread as far as the Ozark Mountains in Arkansas. I am sure I am exaggerating but a church in Mountain Home Arkansas had asked if by some chance we ever got over to Arkansas, please stop in and at least say hello. So we thought why not go to the Ozark Mountains? We had a great time at the church in Mountain Home. We spent three days there enjoying the fellowship with those wonderful people.

Then we took off sightseeing. First we went to Branson Missouri and spent two days there. It was a lot of fun. What we found out however was that in the area of the Ozark Mountains that summer the weather had been terribly dry. So the leaves didn't have much color, they were all just brown. Because of that we decided to take a circle trip home. WE would go by way of the Appellation Mountains. Thru Tennessee, North Carolina and North Georgia. That way we might see some of the beautiful color that we both loved.

It was a long but beautiful trip. On the way home from the mountains we took the route that would bring us through Wrightsville Georgia. That happens to be where Mary was born. She also had some cousins there. We planned to drive all the way home that day but as we were passing through Wrightsville I pulled over to the side of the road. Mary asked "Why are you stopping I thought we were not going to stop in Wrightsville?" "I don't really know why" I answered. "I just somehow felt like I should. Maybe we should set here for a minute." "You know" I said. "We have been to Wrightsville many times and I never thought of it as a pretty area, but for some reason today it is. Would you ever want to live in this part of Georgia?" "I guess it would be ok but I can think of better places," she answered. I just sat there for a minute longer, restarted the car and headed home.

I was back at work two days later and for some reason I called CEF headquarters and asked who would I talk to if I wanted to become a permanent worker for CEF. They directed my call to Moises Estevez. He asked where I was considering to go. When I told him Georgia he was amazed. He said that he had been on the phone with the director of CEF of Georgia less than an hour ago. They had prayed and asked the Lord to send someone to Georgia. What a coincidence. I asked him "what would I have to do to be able to go to Georgia as a missionary for CEF." He said "I have your file in front of me on the computer. If Mary and you want to serve together, both of you would have to get 8 more weeks of school to get the degree you need." Then he said. "It will be up to you to get support, CEF is a faith based ministry." We chatted for a few more minutes and he suggested, "if and when you are ready you should call the director in Georgia."

That's what I did. When I called him and told him what was on my mind he to become excited? "Where in Georgia do you think God is calling you," he asked? When I said Middle Georgia, using Macon as a reference point, He nearly came through the phone. He had just finished hanging up with a man in Macon who was telling him that they needed to send a CEF worker to Macon to get CEF restarted. What a coincidence. We talked for quite a while and agreed to meet in Milledgeville Georgia and talk everything over.

That evening Mary and I talked a lot and we prayed a lot. This was a very big decision. It would mean my quitting a very good job. Our savings were very low at the time. My 401 K was down 60% due to the economy, and I was 60 years old, Mary was 55. Another good reason was that Pan American Airlines had declared bankruptcy just 3 years earlier. They had

Chapter 19

asked the US government to let them spend the employee retirement fund to keep them from going bankrupt but to no avail. So when they went, so did our pensions. I had well over 35 years seniority but no pension. A few good earthly reasons to forget the idea right now, wouldn't you think? One of the reasons was also that we would need $1600.00 dollars each to finish our schooling. We really did not have it right now. So we agreed to think and pray about this for a few days and see how we felt.

I was pulling up to our driveway just 3 days later and as usual I stopped and got out to check the mailbox. When I pulled out the mail there was a letter from, of all people Pan American Airlines. Since they had went bankrupt over 3 years ago I wondered what in the world this was all about. I had to see right then so I opened the letter. Inside was a letter explaining that they were still settling up old accounts and had found an old account of mine that I had put money into for quite a while, then the program had been eliminated. I had forgotten all about it years ago. With the letter was a check for: you guessed it right: $3,200.00 dollars. What a coincidence. I fell on my knees right there at the mailbox and cried. "Dear Heavenly Father Please forgive me for ever doubting you. We will go to Georgia and we will trust you to provide". When I went in and showed the letter and the check to Mary she too was ready to go. One of our very favorite verses from the Bible is, "Faithful is He who calleth you, who also will do it."

There was a lot of things that had to be done before we could go to Georgia including finishing our schooling. We thought that for monies sake we would go to school while I was still working and drawing a salary. I had a plenty of vacation and comp time coming to me. We had already closed the flower shops so that was no problem. I told my employer what I had in mind. They were great about everything. They hated to see me go but they also had known about my work with CEF and they had always understood and approved.

WE drove out to Warrenton this time and finished our requirements in order to become CEF directors in Georgia. I still did not leave SATO right away. We wanted some time to do some deputation work to try and raise some of the support we would need. We were members of Liberty Baptist Church in Orlando Florida. When we told the church of our decision they were indeed excited for us. They voted as a church to be our sending church and to support us as best they could. They also voted and held a service making me a licensed Baptist Minister.

After about 3 months and hundreds and hundreds of miles of deputation later we decided to go. We had lived in Orlando for26 years. We left a lot of good friends behind. We didn't have near the support that we would need. I still don't have it today. But we knew that we could trust God and that everything would be ok. You know what? God has never failed us. What a coincidence.

We first moved to Warner Robins Georgia where the Pastor of Liberty Baptist Church in Warner Robins let us stay in a profits chamber in the church. That church was a true gift from God. We then found and rented a double wide mobile home in Byron Georgia. From there we began to get to work. We advertised in several churches that we would have a Teaching Children Effectively class to be held at Byron Baptist Church in Byron Georgia. We had 6 students attend. From that class we were able to start our first Good News Clubs at Eagle Springs and Byron Elementary School. We were really working missionaries for CEF.

I also began what I consider a very good fair ministry. As of this writing we have attended 16 different fairs here in Macon and in Perry. Between the 20 some different Good News clubs that we have had here in Middle Georgia public schools and the fairs, we have had the wonderful privilege of leading literally thousands to pray for salvation.

We had been praying a lot for God to give us a church to attend as members. What he led us to was Southside Baptist church in Warner Robins. At that time it was a tossup between Southside and Berean Baptist Church in Macon Georgia. I know that one was not better than the other but God led us to Southside. What a great church. There were some problems to overcome. Most of them financial, but amazingly God continued to provide. The years and events rolled by quickly.

Chapter 20

It was Christmas Eve 2004. Mary and I were at the Christmas Eve candle light service at Southside. Mary had mentioned that she didn't feel very good and I had said lets go home. She said "NO I'll be fine."

The next thing I noticed was that she was having difficulty breathing. I said "let's go to the emergency room at the hospital." She would not go so I decided to try and trick her. I said "let's at least go on home and you can put your feet up and maybe you'll feel better," My plan was to get her to the hospital, she agreed to that and we left. Just as she got to our van she passed out. I could not awaken her so I took off as fast as I could to the Houston County Hospital. Mary went home to be with the Lord that night. I like to try and think of it as the best Christmas gift Mary could get. Going home to Heaven on Christmas Eve, but it wasn't for me, I took it very hard. She was my life and I miss her so much. She was my inspiration and my life. Southside Baptist Church was wonderful. The pastor, the people, they all did everything they could to make things easy for me. The pastor went with my son Michael and me to the funeral home to help make the arrangements, then he surprised us by telling the funeral home to send the entire bill to Southside. God is so good! He sure keeps His promises.

It was over a year later and I was still teaching the 6 year old children's Sunday school class. The class Mary and I had taught together. Another Lady had come in to help but her husband had to transfer to Minnesota to keep his job. I was again left alone with an average of 30 kids every Sunday. Just before church service started I had made several remarks about how "I could really use some help in the Sunday school class," loud enough for all of the ladies in widows row to hear me. One of the ladies, a widow,

Mrs. Margaret Murr finally responded. She said that she would help temporarily until I could find a permanent replacement.

In church, as I am sure is true in many churches, we had a so called "widows row" and a "widowers row". This lady, so I was told, had moved from the widow's row to the so called widower's row, but sat on the far end. I had several people tell me later that she had moved a little closer every Sunday until the only thing between us was Mathew, Mark, Luke and John. Believe it or not I really never noticed it. One Sunday she asked me what was I going to do after church? I told her my routine was to go to a chicken restaurant, Mrs. Winners, and get a fried chicken lunch to go, take it home and watch a football game. She asked, "Have you ever gone to Georgia Bob's." Georgia Bob's is a BBQ restaurant? I said "yes I have and it was good." She then asked "would you like to go have lunch at Georgia Bob's with me?" I sort of liked the idea of a little company, and said "yes I would that sounds nice."

I think the way protocol works is that I was supposed to make the next move. I didn't and two weeks went by. Then she said that she had enjoyed having company at lunch and would I go with her for Japanese food after church. I said that I would. I had enjoyed the very good company as well. We went and had a very good time. Well several weeks went by when in the church bulletin there was an invitation for the older members of our church to go to a catfish dinner in Douglas Georgia. A place called the "Catfish House". They were all to meet at the church next Friday evening and take the church bus to Douglas. It sounded like fun and I liked catfish. So I asked Margaret if she wanted to go with me. I told her that I liked catfish but it didn't sound like fun to go alone and be a third wheel. She told me that she liked good catfish as well and it did sound like fun. It was fun and we started getting to know each other better.

It was getting close to Christmas. Not my favorite time of the year. At least not then. Margaret asked me if I wanted to come to her house and have Christmas dinner with her and some of her family. I would have enjoyed myself, I know that. But I had already made plans to go to Orlando and be with my kids. At that time that was more important to me. I didn't know or I guess even think about it, but I almost totally discouraged her by not coming. I can only guess why. But when I got back to Warner Robins and church I asked her to go to lunch with me. She agreed to and it seems from there things began to move more rapidly in our relationship.

Margaret had two children of her own. A daughter Jenifer, who was divorced. And a son Mathew, married. They both have children of their own. Jenifer has a daughter Sally who was an older teenager. Both Jenifer and Sally were living in Margaret's home. Mathew is married to Denise and they have two sons Ron and Able both of them teens, both great boys.

Margaret and I began to see each other more often. One day marriage was brought up and discussed. I wanted her to know up front that if we ever did get married that she was marrying a missionary and if God called me I would go to Africa if that's where he called me. As things became more serious I stressed that point a lot. She said she understood and that God came first in her life as well, it sounded good. The next thing you know we were making wedding plans. We went to the pastor of our church for marriage counseling because I wanted her to be sure she understand what she was getting into. Her responses to him were great. After almost ten years I know why I married Margaret, I can't speak for Margaret, but I did it because I love her.

Our wedding was lovely. We were married at Southside Baptist Church. An assistant pastor whom we had both befriended because of his help with the Good News Clubs that Southside Baptist Church sponsored, performed the ceremony. I told you that we had around 30 children in our Sunday school class, we asked them all to participate by being either flower girls, bell ringers, or ring bearers. They were wonderful. Both of our families participated by being best men or brides maids. Margaret's son Mathew, gave her away. There were lots of flowers and crystal for decoration. I also mentioned my Scottish history, I have always loved "The Pipes", so we had a man playing Amazing Grace at the end of our ceremony on the bag pipes. I believe we were married in style. Anyhow the wedding and the reception was beautiful.

I own a mobile home in Byron and she has a large house in Warner Robins in a nice neighborhood. She wanted to live in her home so I agreed. Jenifer and Sally did move out after a while. And Sally now has a man she lives with and two beautiful little girls, Abby and Kendall, two more Great grandchildren.

Chapter 21

There is another situation that I want to share with you. We were starting a Good News Club in a school that I will not name, because the principal of that school did not want us in that school. When we had originally met with the principal and the pastor of the sponsoring church and everything seemed fine. However when we started the club it changed. The principal did everything possible to make it difficult for us. With God's help the club still did well. Our Good News clubs have twelve weeks of one series of lessons and then if you want you start another series. The workers chose to start a second twelve weeks. To do this I had to do another mail out to the parents. The club was on Thursday at 3:30pm, at 6pm on Wednesday I received a call from the principal telling me that I better not show up because they thought that what we were doing was illegal and I would need the approval of the school board to come back. I tried reason, explaining that the board knew that we were legal as the United States Supreme Court had decided that long ago. The phone went dead. There was no one at the school board at 6:00 pm on Wednesday, so at 9:00 am Thursday I was on the phone to the school board. I asked to speak to the assistant superintendent and was told he was not available, I got an appointment for 2:30 pm. I explained that I was going to be at the school by 3:30pm because there were 35 kids there that the parents were certainly not expecting to be abandoned. We were at the school board office by 2:00 pm. While I was waiting I was praying, I mean I was praying hard for God to help us. Just then my cell phone rang. It was a legal aid from Liberty Counsel in Virginia. He gave his name and told me that their boss had taken them to lunch today and while at lunch he had turned to me and said "There is a man in Georgia that's been on my mind all day. His name is Frank Tracy and he is the local director for CEF in Middle Georgia. When you get back to the office call and ask him if everything is ok." When I told the legal aid why and where we were he was amazed. He told me "keep your phone handy we'll call you right back." Just then the assistant superintendent and their in house attorney came up and introduced themselves to us. As we were going into their office my phone rang again, I asked them please excuse me, that I had to take this call, It was an attorney from Liberty Counsel. Let me interject here that I had not contacted or spoken to anyone at Liberty Counsel for at least three years. The attorney from Liberty Council asked me what was going on at the moment, I briefly explained, and then he said "give your phone to the attorney." I did, and in just a minute the whole attitude in that office changed. The school attorney then handed the phone back to me. The Liberty attorney told me to get on over to the school and call him back on the way and he would explain the conversation between him and the school attorney. As I hung up the school board attorney told me to go on to the school and everything would be ok. I mentioned that the principal at the school might still give us a hard time. I was assured that would not happen. From that day on we have never had a problem in that school again. God was not only there the day we needed Him, or the hour, He was there the very moment we needed Him. What a coincidence

At this point in our marriage; Margaret is 75 and I am 73, we have a lot of physical problems. Margaret has had a second neck and spinal surgery, it seems to have gone well. She also has neuropathy in her feet. Her feet hurt pretty much all of the time. Just a few weeks ago she was diagnosed with pre Diabetes.

I am certainly not without a few problems. I have a very bad back and have a lot of trouble standing very long or walking any distance at all. I am right now contemplating surgery. I also have a little heart murmur but I take pills for that. I do have a chronic breathing condition, COPD, but I can handle that ok.

I have no doubt that my Father in Heaven put us together in our old age for the purpose of helping one another. I will do my best to do what I believe God wants me to do. One of the hardest things for me to learn is patience, I'm working on it. But at 73? I have always said that for

Chapter 21

me to have patience I would have to be a doctor. I also said that I love Margaret, and I do.

You are by now asking, what about your little brother and sister. I got together with them almost 14 years after we were torn apart. I had found out that my mother was still in Davenport Iowa and so was my little sister. Mary and I flew into Moline and drove over to Davenport to see if my mother wanted to come and live a while with us. I tried to reconcile with my mother but I don't think our lifestyles matched up very well, so my attempts were, at best partially effective. I thought she might enjoy being around her grandchildren. She did come to Miami, stayed about three months and one day she was gone again. I do not know exactly when or why my father passed away. While in Davenport I was able to spend a lot of time with Molly. That gave me a chance to know my nephews and my niece. We had a great time. There were a lot of tears and some laughs. Molly was working for Oscar Meyer and was doing well. From Molly I was able to locate my brother Billy. He was able to come with his wife to Miami and stay with us for a few months. This gave Billy and me a chance to get to know one another again. It turns out that Billy was about to become a professional student. When he came to Miami he had already gotten at least two degrees and did some work and study at the University of Miami for another degree. He has studied and taught at so many Universities that I have lost track. I know he got a PHD at Stanford. I don't want tell too much because I intend to write another book or two.

I would like to at this point add that my mother and father have passed away, also my older brother Richard. Richard was 52 and died of cardiomyopathy.

There is still a lot of work to do.

Many names have been changed to protect the privacy of everyone.

www.ingramcontent.com/pod-product-compliance
Ingram Content Group UK Ltd.
Pitfield, Milton Keynes, MK11 3LW, UK
UKHW022220230426
12048UKWH00016BA/970